POETRY INDEX

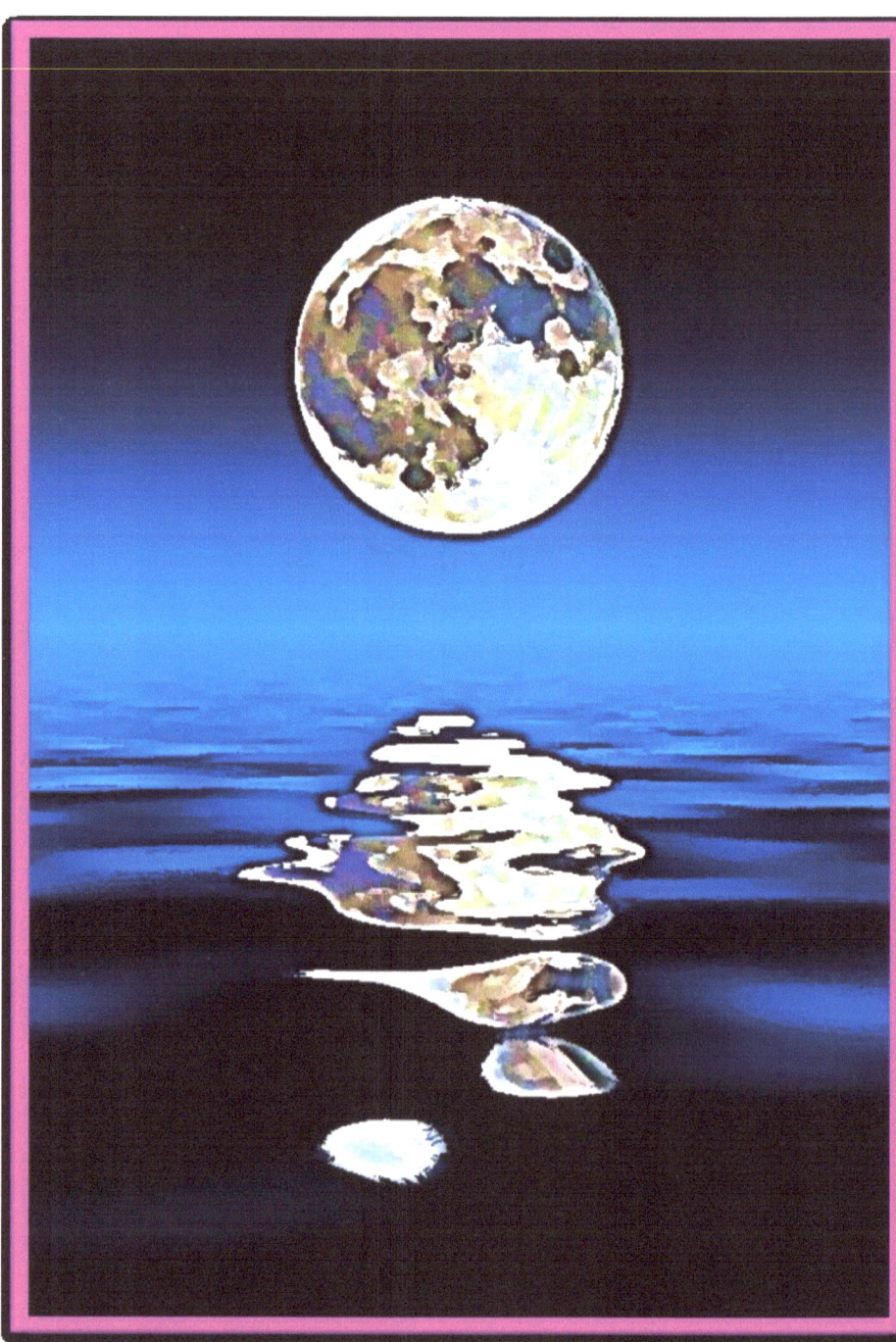

Pink Ocean

My lips cling
to soft contoured lines of pinkness.
Apollo ascends through pale colored skin
wondering if you notice.
My slate has chalky markings
of shellfish dust fading.
Here we are
experience divided,
two separate spectrums of one's journey and one's goal.

Readiness longs to inject
and arrival's gut knows.
Stained crimson and muddied pearl
cleansed by immaculate perception.
Knowing our desire,
Neptune's palette's aroused
by nether wishes,
to swim forever undisturbed,
in our pink ocean.

Chicago Scent

My city basement with Chicago scent
and a concrete backyard with cracks in it;
the backdoor staircase with smooth grey paint
I ran up and down until dusk called my name.

A knock on Johnny's door, signaling him,
racing each other to see who's faster,
unleashing energy bound inside us.
Our limbs filled with nature's first green of gold.

The yell of some mothers voice, calling out,
checking her chick out of obligation;
her voice faint, blocked by bricks of city life,
waiting to hear her annoyed one yell,"What"!

The hours of days seeming like minutes
not wanting pretend to end with twilight,
as brown and blue eyes fade with sunset's glow,
hoping 'morrow will bring sameness, newness.

The easiness of seven, eight, or nine
will live forever in a thousand footsteps,
on grey stairs, cracked cement, tall urban trees
and city pavement with Chicago scent.

Mommy's Arms

Her twins were born
no man was there
no man to care, though mommy's here.

One in each arm
two perfect charms
with nights so long, they make her strong.

Mommy's a peach
but is tough as nails
her twins come first before her thirst.

It's oh so hard
to raise these babes
but it's worth the wait of her twin's true fate.

These babes grow big
as mommy strives
to guide the lives of four deep blue eyes.

These twins now grown
their beauty's shown
because mommy's arms were strong as stone.

Subconscious Zone

Does anybody listen? Is it selfish intuition?
The words flow from my mouth to ear
but my words seem all too much to bear.
What scares me even more than this
is maybe people care not one bit.
They're all caught up in a crazy world
which makes me want to crawl up and curl.
Deep down I know that people hear
the truth denied grows out of fear.
This truth denied somehow they know
but just can't deal with their subconscious zone.
I deal with this zone so well
that's why I shout it to the crowd.
This zone so loud one has to know
is evident for life to flow.
Resist it and you'll find one day
the dead zone comes then there's no way!

To Shine or Not to Shine

They don't want me to shine.
They'd rather hear me whine.
'Cause if I shine the light's too bright
and makes their minds go blind.
It started long ago as my light began to grow.
They wouldn't understand the light I chose to throw.
I threw it anyway, and some considered play.
The power filled me up, until their clouds took it away.
Some still choose cold than warm,
as jealously controls their form,
yet it will only fade away, as my light gets in their way.
I understand their fears, as ego grabs and tears,
but is it right, to take the light
of someone's fate, who dares?
Some will open their minds, while others run and hide.
But the ones who chose my light will only shine more bright.

Going To See Grandma

I liked taking the bus to see grandma.
I was only nine but mom gave good instructions.
I'd meet grandma after 5 o'clock mass. We'd always
walk to the neighborhood restaurant and have patty
melts. They were so tasty, smothered with cheese and
onions. Grandma always let me have a second coke while
she drank tea. Afterwards we'd walk to the nearby candy
store and buy mnm's. I'd hold grandma's hand and look up
at her on our walk home. Her bright red lipstick popped
against her powdered skin. Het silk white dress with blue
jays on it blew in the wind. She looked just like a grandma
should look. Once we got to grandma's bungalow we'd
settle in for the night. Grandma would put on her
housedress and finish her chores. I'd play in the tub for a
while and then put on my jammies. Later, we'd watch the
Carol Burnett show. I'd sit on the floor next to Grandma's
chair laughing and munching on mnm's. When the show
was over it was time for bed. Grandma would tuck me into
Grandpa's big mahogany bed. He was in heaven.
The sheets were fresh and crisp with a faint scent of
mothballs. I'd say a prayer and fall right to sleep.
I'm sure I dreamt.

MADONNA

I started from nothing, didn't know which way to go.

New York was the answer to put on my show.

No time to waste, the beginning of a new race;

revolutionary destination of the brightest innovation.

At my insistence the time had come for my existence.

I knew how to do it; you see my brilliance diffused resistance.

The right eye caught me. I had finally made it.

I was seen by the world which was the stage I had created.

Music is my statement which is polished and designed.

My music has conviction and a reason to survive.

Though much more than survival is the real question at hand.

The answer to this venture is the hunger to command.

Unseen Creatures

A pine branch bounces in airy display
not from the wind, but from exotic limbs
absent of humanistic quality
present in alien nature and guise.

Pointed needles release scented splendor
attracting creatures unseen to the eye
felt by hearts tuned to nature's purest grip
possessing instinctiveness to guide them.

A silent bark unheard by human ears
roughened by years of earthly elements
entrances esurient specimens
ready for a gulp of exaltation.

Microscopic legs dig with fierce freedom
as keen senses search for what is hidden
dissolving in a familiar haven
waiting for a touch that incites comfort.

Once this taste penetrates a beating heart
a steadiness sets an absolute tone
which binds the unseen in its own world
allowing for growth and new beginnings.

The Topic

I confront you, you don't like it, want to hear it, want to deal with it. I understand the topic's pressing and the feeling so insisting. You know by now my words can't help but engage strong reinforcement. If I don't act it's sort of useless which makes us separate, somewhat distant. Please don't avoid the simple concept that communication is the object. It's true personas sometimes clash but shouldn't kill the final act. I have a feeling you'd agree that certain topics cause some steam. We both know steam enlarges pores of evolutionary doors. So why not open your mind completely and climb the next step much more swiftly. You know my words aren't meant to hurt you, but instill a growing virtue. By now I've spoken loud and clear, I hope erasing all the fear. So let us now both work together in pursuit of a lasting future.

IF HE KNEW DEATH

Sonnet

Would life be easier if he knew death
ascension to heaven would he feel free
a life of questions all answered, non-left
a truthfulness complete unknown to thee?

Once young he knew not of a hollow end
expecting his flesh to remain intact
a year was a day, forever his friend
free as the wind with no weight on his back.

A man all grown now does wonder what comes
much wiser of course from a past observed
knowing the future he can't escape from
awaiting peace from a puzzle still blurred.

There is one answer this human may give.
A life not yet solved, won't stop until lived.

I hear her dance

Sonnet

Her movements are liquid fluidity
that I have only seen but never heard.
My heart pulsates with utter certainty
as limbs flow in almost airy absurd.

Bright lights make her image sheer and ghostly,
conspicuously illusionistic.
"Moonlight Sonata" propels mastery
through a body designed altruistic.

Glissando penetrates me through her steps
while ascending to my fearless eardrums,
begging the beat to permeate my depth
so I may hear a prowess never shunned.

True, my ears may not heed through eyes entranced.
So we become one, and I hear her dance.

THIS PATH

Looking down this path, I see what fate awaits me.
Every step I make brings me closer to the real me.
This me I call real is what I always wanted.
Hoping time holds on until I've all but rusted.
Every step I take solidifies my certainty
keeping my eyes peeled looking right into my destiny.
My steps not always firm, but worthy of the strength it takes
knowing that each step has knowledge of my past mistakes.
From youth I've always known this path was one long magnet
pulling me much closer to my entitled pageant.
At times it's dark and foggy and the lightning tries to strike me,
so I put on my armor and let my senses guide me.
Sometimes it's crystal clear and I see the blazing sun,
and know the day will come when I meet my own horizon.
This path I've strolled till now has footprints of an awkward one,
which shows me time well spent has ripened the now polished one.
These steps that I foresee are laced with brilliant circuitry.
So this path shall continue and lead me to sweet victory.

The Craven Father

His twins were born
he wasn't there
he didn't care,
a craven's fear.

His flesh and blood
he threw away
so he could play
his foolish games.

No morals inside
just selfish pride
narcissistically gliding
through his visionless life.

It boggles my mind
that a man who's a father
would so easily dismiss
the beauty of this power.

The ability to mold,
facility to care,
empathy to love,
the capability to share.

He broke his twin's hearts
split them right in two
they've mended by now
but the scars still show through.

He's our Man

Curvy, hard, and fertile
strong, entrenched and virile

He knows what he has

Sweating for hours on end
pushing his motives ahead

He sees fantasy become reality

His presence primed and sleek
while eyes do sneak a peek

He knows they're watching

Living life on the edge
whispering thoughts on their ledge

He knows they hear him

Fastened and ready to go
it's time to put on his show

He hears them calling

The One

Is there a man I will meet
that will sweep me off my feet?
I fantasize of that man and wonder
when he'll touch my hand.
In my mind I visualize that perfect gaze which meets my eyes.
Every time I see that gaze it's out of reach for I'm afraid.
The chance has come from time to time
though my mind defends that fragile child.
I'm all grown up physically
but not so much emotionally.
Two years to go before 3-0
I hope my hand will touch him so.
If no one comes before that day
then waiting has to be the way.
I will not settle none the less,
for I deserve the very best.
If best waits long to come my way,
oh well, I'll live, I'll love, I'll play.

Heath

Sonnet

A patriot in early youth was he
abandoning beauty over substance.
Defiantly kind and blind he might be
unaware of turbulent circumstance.

Accolades would shape and build his bosom
cradling a heart filled with fervent reason
while golden curly tides sway favor some
through a breathy jungle's freakish season.

Red becomes the replacement of pavement
a cushion for hemlines and prominence.
But he only feels the icy cement
waving his hand with arrant radiance

A joker's eyes are his last tasty treat
in a place called "OZ" paved in golden streets.

This Little Guy

This little guy, he asks why the bigger ones want him to fry.

He struggles with an attitude so indifferent and clearly rude.

This little guy won't run away, he'll take a stand; make sure

they pay .But the bigger ones will block the view of this little

guy who knows the truth. He scrapes and chips and feels the

pain of bigger ones abrasive chains, but this little guys heart

and soul will melt these chains of ice so cold. The day will

come when the bigger ones will know the pain of this little

guy, and the chains that once had frozen him will now freeze

every one of them. When the bigger ones now chained and

cold regret the actions they once sold this little guy no doubt

all grown now does become the bigger one.

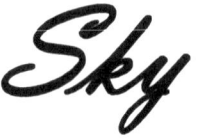

The sky soft and simple

A world above the earth and below the heavens

mirroring the fluid sea along a path of tranquility

A chamber of colors represents it's most secret emotions

Unpredictable, alive, though at the same time silent

Telling its vivid story with infinite meaning.

Punk

He asked me what the term "punk" meant.

A euphemism used in the book "To kill a mocking bird".

I knew he did it on purpose. Was it to embarrass me?

There were 29 other kids in the class. Why ask me?

He wanted, for some reason to expose me.

I gave him the right answer, though derogatory.

When I answered, they all laughed, including him.

I was fifteen, my defense mechanisms kicked in.

My outsides showed the smugness of an answer they all

laughed at. Inside I felt tested, targeted and betrayed.

I think I grew up about five years in five minutes.

What was obvious to me wasn't to the others.

I seemed I pulled it off. The experience was a negative

defining moment in my life. A moment where the stickiness

has to dry before one can wash it off. I washed it off all

right; until I sparkled. There's no way I'd let this small time

English teacher break me. I was smarter than him.

After the answer I gave, he knew it.

Mom's Green Eye Shadow

Acrostic Poem

Mom was asleep in the living room
on a lazy Sunday afternoon
murmuring with a smile on her face;
sunbeams shining, going "peek-a-boo."

Green was the color I picked
right smack out of the seventies.
Even strokes across her eyes,
equal to that of iridescent emeralds,
nuances refined with subtle easiness.

Eight years old and already an artist
young hands trying to perfect
Eventful for such a novice mind.
Smoothing out each crease meticulously
hoping that when her lids would open she'd say,
"Ah, at last I awake from a pleasant dream
delighted by a vision that radiates viridty
only to show that my hazel gems
win over the creatures of the world."

Gisele

Sonnet

Gisele Bundchen is a fashion queen

strutting her glory in couture fashion.

No gems compare to those eyes ever green;

not the sun nor moon may breed such passion.

Glamorous fabrics adorn her soft skin

as colored palettes perfect each feature.

The wind in her hair is void of all sin

forgiving beauty's alluring creature.

Blond legs stride by invitation only

greeted by scents from Chanel to Dior.

Her stare is a greeting, never lonely

A crowd so bewitched screaming "more oh more"!

Oh Gisele may you feverishly sway!

Amorously taking our breaths' away!

In her sixties

She's in her sixties and does what she wants.
Watch a movie, read a book, drink some wine
maybe even cook.
There's no rules now
Paid her dues and how.
It's more than ok, its friggen allowed.
She's gotta routine,
happens when ya get older
don't want the hassle
it's time to relax and all.
She's got her gran kids and keeps in touch.
Wishes they were closer
but for now it's good enough.
Yeah, she's in her sixties; alone and likes it.
No man to bother with, keepin it comfortable and
private.
Somethins always gonna happen.
Somethins always goin down.
So far she's gone the distance.
With still sa'more to come.

He has HIV

SONNET

He has HIV was it meant to be?
He got it real young, a question for some.
T'was not ignorance that caused the unseen;
Simply emptiness from being so numb.

An organ of love was fractured by death
as a heart tries to mend torment endured.
Living in limbo, no care with each breath.
The veins of this one quite honest and pure.

Excuses are easy until a day
When one takes a looks at a past observed.
A face in the mirror has a new display
as life forces out a backbone with nerve.

It's all too easy to sink in abyss.
Will he stay afloat on strength that exists?

YELLOW TEARS

A bunch of tears my eyes do weep
on yellow petals of daises in full bloom.
For when the rainfall comes
I shower them with salted thoughts.
My yellow friends gesture amorously
embracing my liquidity.
After the cascade, they're all dewy,
and glisten with memories of moments ago.
I stare into those yellow tears
and fall into their world,
absorbing the abstractions I just poured.
Yellow petals chant in soiled tongue
as I journey through watery lands.
I feel safe and warm in their tame sea
protected from reality's taste.
Though the sun shines through
and I must swim my way back.
Beckoning for my return, I assure them;
There will always be more yellow tears.

Beauty Captured

Sonnet

Lingering beauty my mirror does capture
An angle I glance from, slight depiction
Realizing time is always the master
Smoothing out cracks that time's clock has shifted.
Seizing the moments, charging much faster
Catching my breath now, clenched and tightfisted
Keeping eyes glued, avoiding the blaster.

Getting much closer, checking my docket
A thoughtful process, guessing my outcome
Seeking out paths which will test my project
Knowing my actions create true stardom
Assuming my stance, aligned and erect
The pace moving fast, true phenomenon
Beauty's knowledge, I'm told by the prophet.

DOMAIN

Protected by dark sunglasses, a half smile and black fiberglass
his domain awaits.
From element of air to element of solitude expects,
rooms mismatched, seeing nothing,
Everything.
Shadows of former bits, all knowing, seize pores
ungratified, tightening.
Wasted time pushing hands to wasted life
Worse yet, wasted heart.
Ivory colored walls bathe in hope's obsolescence
contrasting colors of cabernet sips.
A through Z feels familiar fingertips
A boxy friend of empty flesh.
Every word is bankrupt of emotion
that all five rooms breathe.
Solitudes iron jaws favor him
A dawn's enemy.
Stained lips and careless legs retreat to one room
where thought has no place
and no reason.

www.ingramcontent.com/pod-product-compliance
Lightning Source LLC
Chambersburg PA
CBHW042348200526
45159CB00034BA/881